VEGAN
cookies

ICE HOUSE BOOKS

Published by Ice House Books

Copyright © 2020 Ice House Books

Compiled by Zulekhá Afzal & Raphaella Thompson
Designed by Emily Curtis

Ice House Books is an imprint of Half Moon Bay Limited
The Ice House, 124 Walcot Street, Bath, BA1 5BG
www.icehousebooks.co.uk

ISBN 978-1-912867-87-5

Printed in China

TO:

....

FROM:

....

contents

CLASSIC
VANILLA
shortbread

Makes approx. 20
Prep 10 minutes, plus 1 hour chilling
Cook 12–15 minutes

Ingredients

200 g (7 oz) vegan butter
100 g (3½ oz) caster sugar, plus extra for sprinkling
1 tsp vanilla extract
300 g (10½ oz) plain flour

Method

1. In a large mixing bowl, cream together the vegan butter and sugar. Add the vanilla extract and sift in the flour. Mix until smooth and it forms a dough. Cover the bowl in vegan food wrap and refrigerate for one hour.

2. Preheat the oven to 180°C/160°C fan/gas 4 and line a baking tray with greaseproof paper.

3. Once the dough has chilled, roll it out to approximately ½ cm–1 cm thick. Use a round or fluted cookie cutter to cut out the shapes.

4. Put the shortbread cookies on the baking tray, leaving space between each one, and sprinkle over a little extra caster sugar.

5. Bake until golden-brown, for approximately 12–15 minutes. Enjoy warm or allow to cool on a wire rack, then tuck in.

CHEWY COCONUT *cookies*

Makes approx. 20
Prep 10 minutes
Cook 12 minutes

Ingredients

110 g (3¾ oz) vegan butter
200 g (7 oz) caster sugar
½ tsp vanilla extract
½ tsp coconut extract
150 g (5¼ oz) plain flour

Ingredients cont.

½ tsp bicarbonate of soda
pinch of salt
100 g (3½ oz) desiccated coconut
2–4 tbsp plant-based milk

Method

1. Preheat the oven to 180°C/160°C fan/gas 4 and line a baking tray with greaseproof paper.

2. In a large bowl, cream the vegan butter and sugar together. Add the vanilla and coconut extracts and give everything a mix.

3. In a separate bowl, sift in the flour and add the bicarbonate of soda, salt and desiccated coconut. Mix then add the dry ingredients to the butter and sugar mixture. Use your hands to mix all the ingredients until a crumbly texture forms.

4. Stir in one tablespoon of plant-based milk. Continue adding the milk, one tablespoon at a time, until the dough comes together enough to roll into balls.

5. Take tablespoon-sized amounts of the mixture and roll into balls, then flatten slightly. Place the cookies on the baking tray.

6. Bake for approximately 12 minutes until the edges are firm and the middle is still soft. Allow to cool on a wire rack and enjoy.

A balanced
diet is a
cookie in
each hand.

Barbara Johnson

YESTERDAY, I REALLY FANCIED COOKIES. TODAY, I'M EATING COOKIES. *Follow your dreams!*

BAKED
ORANGE
cookies

Makes approx. 20
Prep 20 minutes
Cook 10–12 minutes

Ingredients

100 g (3½ oz) vegan butter
100 g (3½ oz) caster sugar
2 tsp grated orange peel
1 tsp vanilla extract
130 g (4½ oz) plain flour
½ tsp bicarbonate of soda
pinch of salt

Method

1. Preheat the oven to 180°C/160°C fan/gas 4 and line a baking tray with greaseproof paper.

2. In a large bowl, cream together the vegan butter and sugar. Beat in the orange peel and vanilla extract until combined.

3. Sift together the flour, bicarbonate of soda and salt into another large bowl. Add the dry mixture to the butter mixture and stir until thoroughly combined.

4. Take tablespoon-sized amounts of the mixture and roll into balls. Arrange them on a baking tray, flattening slightly.

5. Bake for 10–12 minutes, until golden-brown.

6. Remove from the oven and allow the cookies to cool on a wire rack. Yummy!

GINGER *snaps*

Makes approx. 20
Prep 20 minutes
Cook 12 minutes

Ingredients

30 g (1 oz) vegan butter
100 g (3½ oz) soft brown sugar
40 g (1½ oz) molasses
¼ tsp vanilla extract
125 g (4½ oz) plain flour
½ tsp bicarbonate of soda
pinch of salt
1 tsp ground ginger
1 tsp ground cinnamon

Ingredients cont.

¼ tsp allspice
¼ tsp ground cloves
1–2 tbsp plant-based milk
25 g (¾ oz) granulated sugar, for rolling

Method

1. Preheat the oven to 180°C/160°C fan/gas 4
   and line a baking tray with greaseproof paper.

2. In a large bowl, cream together the vegan butter
   and sugar. Stir in the molasses and vanilla extract.

3. In another bowl, sift together the flour, bicarbonate
   of soda, salt, ground ginger, cinnamon, allspice and
   cloves. Stir well then add the dry mixture to the butter
   mixture. Mix by hand until a crumbly texture forms.

4. Add the plant-based milk and mix until it comes
   together to form a soft dough.

5. Take tablespoon-sized amounts of the mixture
   and roll into balls. Roll the balls in the sugar.

6. Place the balls on the baking tray, with a little
   space between them, and flatten slightly.

7. Bake for 12 minutes (or 10 minutes if you're after
   a chewier cookie), then allow the cookies to cool
   on a wire rack. Now it's time to get stuck in.

NO-BAKE PEANUT BUTTER *cookies*

Makes approx. 20
Prep 10 minutes
Cook 5–10 minutes, plus 15 minutes chilling

Ingredients

6 tbsp maple syrup
2½ tbsp plant-based milk
4 tbsp coconut oil
4 tbsp cocoa powder
225 g (8 oz) rolled oats
55 g (2 oz) natural crunchy peanut butter
¾ tsp vanilla extract
pinch of salt
95 g (3½ oz) vegan dark chocolate, chopped

Method

1. Line a baking tray with greaseproof paper.

2. In a medium pan over a medium heat, mix together the maple syrup, plant-based milk, coconut oil and cocoa powder.

3. Once bubbling, allow to boil for one minute then remove from the heat. Mix in the rolled oats, peanut butter, vanilla extract, salt and dark chocolate until fully incorporated.

4. Take tablespoon-sized amounts of the mixture and spoon onto the baking tray.

5. Pop in the fridge and allow to cool and harden for 15 minutes. Enjoy!

SNICKER *doodles*

Makes approx. 15
Prep 20 minutes
Cook 15 minutes

Ingredients

30 g (1 oz) coconut oil
10 tbsp maple syrup
4 tbsp plant-based milk
1 tsp vanilla extract
150 g (5¼ oz) ground almonds

Ingredients cont.

150 g (5¼ oz) plain flour
1 tsp baking powder
2 tsp ground cinnamon
3 tbsp coconut sugar

Method

1. Preheat the oven to 180°C/160°C fan/gas 4
   and line a baking tray with greaseproof paper.

2. Melt the coconut oil in a pan on a low heat, then
   add the maple syrup, plant-based milk and vanilla
   extract. Mix to combine.

3. Remove the bowl from the heat and add the
   ground almonds, flour and baking powder.
   Mix until thoroughly incorporated.

4. Mix the cinnamon and coconut sugar together
   and put it in a shallow bowl or baking tray.

5. Take tablespoon-sized amounts of the dough,
   roll into a ball then coat in the cinnamon and
   coconut sugar mixture. Arrange on a baking
   tray(s) and press lightly to flatten.

6. Bake for approximately 15 minutes until
   golden-brown. Once baked, allow to cool
   on a wire rack. It's time to eat.

Cookies are made of [vegan] butter and love.

Norwegian Proverb

WHY WERE THE COOKIES CRYING?

Because their mum was a wafer so long!

CARROT CAKE *cookies*

Makes approx. 16
Prep 20 minutes
Cook 15 minutes

Ingredients

30 g (1 oz) coconut oil
4 tbsp maple syrup
1/2 tsp ground ginger
1 tsp mixed spice
1 tsp vanilla extract
pinch of salt
100 g (3½ oz) carrots, grated
2 tbsp desiccated coconut
25 g (¾ oz) walnuts, chopped
60 g (2 oz) ground almonds
150 g (5¼ oz) rolled oats
250 ml (8¾ fl oz) plant-based milk

Method

1. Preheat the oven to 180°C/160°C fan/gas 4
   and line a baking tray with greaseproof paper.

2. Melt the coconut oil in a pan on a low heat.
   Once melted, remove from the heat and mix in
   the other ingredients, until a doughy texture forms.

3. Take tablespoon-sized amounts of the mixture, roll
   into balls, flattening slightly on the baking tray.

4. Bake for approx. 15 minutes until golden-brown,
   allow to cool on a wire rack, and enjoy.

CHOC CHIP
cookies
(GF)

Makes approx. 12
Prep 15 minutes
Cook 10 minutes

Ingredients

90 g (3 oz) pitted dates
pinch of salt
3 tbsp smooth nut butter
60 g (2 oz) ground almonds
40 g (1½ oz) vegan chocolate chips

Method

1. Preheat the oven to 180°C/160°C fan/gas 4
   and line a baking tray with greaseproof paper.

2. Blend the dates in a food processor until smooth.
   Add the salt, nut butter and ground almonds.
   Mix well then stir in the chocolate chips.

3. Take tablespoon-sized amounts of the cookie
   dough, roll into balls and flatten slightly on the
   baking tray.

4. Bake for 10–12 minutes until golden-brown.
   Allow to cool on a wire rack (if you can resist),
   then tuck in.

PISTACHIO
ROSEWATER
cookies

Makes approx. 12
Prep 15 minutes
Cook 15 minutes

Ingredients

2 tbsp pistachios, shelled
60 g (2 oz) vegan butter
45 g (1½ oz) caster sugar
150 g (5¼ oz) plain flour
½ tsp baking powder
2 tbsp brown rice syrup
2 tsp rosewater

Method

1. Preheat the oven to 180°C/160°C fan/gas 4
   and line a baking tray with greaseproof paper.

2. Put the pistachios in a food processor or blender
   and pulse until finely ground.

3. In a large bowl, cream together the vegan butter
   and sugar until smooth. Sift in the flour and baking
   powder, and mix until combined.

4. Add the rice syrup and rosewater and mix until a
   smooth dough forms. Fold in the ground pistachios.

5. Take tablespoon-sized amounts of the dough, roll
   into balls and slightly flatten on the baking tray.

6. Bake the cookies for approximately 15 minutes
   or until they're golden-brown. Allow to cool
   then try not to eat them in 30 seconds flat.

PEANUT BUTTER *cookies*

Makes approx. 20
Prep 15 minutes
Cook 10 – 12 minutes

Ingredients

250 g (8¾ oz) natural smooth peanut butter
150 g (5¼ oz) coconut sugar
110 ml (3¾ fl oz) almond milk
1 tsp vanilla extract
120 g (4¼ oz) plain flour
1 tsp bicarbonate of soda
pinch of salt

Method

1. Preheat the oven to 180°C/160°C fan/gas 4 and line a baking tray with greaseproof paper.

2. Combine the peanut butter and sugar in a large bowl until creamy. Stir in the almond milk and vanilla extract.

3. Sift the flour and bicarbonate of soda into a separate bowl. Mix in the salt then add the dry ingredients to the wet ingredients and mix until combined. (If the dough is tough, use your hands to mix until combined.)

4. Take tablespoon-sized amounts of the mixture and roll into balls. Arrange them on the baking tray then use the back of a spoon to flatten the balls and create a criss-cross pattern.

5. Bake for 10–12 minutes then allow to cool on a wire rack. It's cookie time!

I'VE MASTERED THE ART OF *procrasti-baking.*

RAISINS THAT LOOK LIKE CHOCOLATE CHIPS ARE THE REASON I HAVE *cookie trust issues.*

WHITE CHOCOLATE CHIP AND SALTED CARAMEL *cookies*

Makes approx. 24
Prep 10 minutes
Cook 7–10 minutes

Ingredients

115 g (4 oz) vegan butter
220 g (7¾ oz) soft brown sugar
½ tsp vanilla extract
3 tbsp plant-based milk
150 g (5¼ oz) plain flour
½ tsp cornflour
½ tsp bicarbonate of soda
pinch of salt
50 g (1¾ oz) vegan white chocolate chips
50 g (1¾ oz) caramel pieces

Method

1. Preheat the oven to 200°C/180°C fan/gas 6 and line a baking tray with greaseproof paper.

2. In a large bowl, cream together the vegan butter and sugar. Mix in the vanilla extract and plant-based milk.

3. In a separate mixing bowl, sift together the flour, cornflour, bicarbonate of soda and salt. Mix in the white chocolate and caramel pieces, then add the dry ingredients to the butter mix, mixing until combined.

4. Take tablespoon-sized amounts of the mixture and roll into balls, flattening slightly. Place the cookies on the baking tray.

5. Bake for 7–10 minutes or until golden-brown. Allow the cookies to cool on a wire rack, make yourself a cuppa, and dunk away.

DOUBLE CHOCOLATE *cookies*

Makes approx. 16
Prep 20 minutes
Cook 10 minutes

Ingredients

115 g (4 oz) vegan butter
100 g (3½ oz) caster sugar
100 g (3½ oz) soft brown sugar
1 tsp vanilla extract
125 g (4½ oz) plain flour
55 g (2 oz) cocoa powder
1 tsp bicarbonate of soda
pinch of salt
1 tbsp plant-based milk
100 g (3½ oz) vegan dark chocolate, finely chopped

Method

1. Preheat the oven to 180°C/160°C fan/gas 4
   and line a baking tray with greaseproof paper.

2. In a large bowl, cream together the vegan butter
   and two sugars. Mix in the vanilla extract.

3. In a separate bowl, sift together the flour and cocoa
   powder. Mix in the bicarbonate of soda and salt.

4. Add the dry ingredients to the wet ingredients and
   mix by hand, until crumbly. Add the plant-based
   milk and mix until it comes together to form a dough.
   Stir in the vegan dark chocolate.

5. Take tablespoon-sized amounts of the mixture
   and roll into balls, then press to flatten slightly.
   Place the cookies on the baking tray.

6. Bake for 10 minutes until the cookie edges are firm,
   but the insides are still soft. Allow the cookies to cool
   on a wire rack, then indulge.

SIMPLE
OATMEAL
cookies

Makes approx. 15
Prep 20 minutes
Cook 15 minutes

Ingredients

145 g (5 oz) rolled oats
125 g (4½ oz) plain flour
80 g (2¾ oz) desiccated coconut
1 tsp bicarbonate of soda
pinch of salt
½ tsp ground cinnamon
115 g (4 oz) vegan butter

Ingredients cont.

200 g (7 oz) soft brown sugar
1 tbsp golden syrup
1 tsp vanilla extract
3 tbsp raisins
1 tbsp plant-based milk

Method

1. Preheat the oven to 180°C/160°C fan/gas 4
   and line a baking tray with greaseproof paper.

2. In a large bowl, mix together the rolled oats, flour,
   coconut, bicarbonate of soda, salt and cinnamon
   until combined.

3. In another bowl, cream together the vegan butter
   and sugar. Mix in the golden syrup and vanilla
   extract until combined.

4. Add the dry ingredients to the wet ingredients
   and mix until just combined. Add the raisins
   and mix in by hand until the mixture is crumbly.

5. Stir in the plant-based milk until the mixture is
   sticky and can roll into a ball.

6. Take tablespoon-sized amounts of the dough and
   roll into balls, arranging them on the baking tray
   and pressing lightly to flatten.

7. Bake for approximately 15 minutes until the cookie
   edges are firm and the tops are slightly brown.
   Allow to cool on a wire rack and enjoy.

PEPPERMINT CRINKLE *cookies*

Makes approx. 20
Prep 20 minutes,
plus 4 hours chilling
Cook 12 minutes

Ingredients

140 g (5 oz) plain flour
70 g (2½ oz) cocoa powder
1½ tsp baking powder
pinch of salt
200 g (7 oz) sugar
1 tbsp apple sauce

Ingredients cont.

1 tbsp vegetable oil
¼ tsp vanilla extract
¼ tsp peppermint extract
55 g (2 oz) icing sugar for coating

Method

1. In a bowl, mix together the flour, cocoa powder, baking powder and salt.

2. In another bowl, mix together the remaining ingredients until well combined. Add the flour mixture and stir until just combined.

3. Cover the bowl in vegan food wrap and chill in the fridge for four hours.

4. Preheat the oven to 180°C/160°C fan/gas 4 and line a baking tray with greaseproof paper.

5. Once chilled, take tablespoon-sized balls of the cookie mixture. Toss the balls in the icing sugar, making sure they are fully coated.

6. Flatten the balls slightly on the baking tray.

7. Bake for approximately 12 minutes, allow to cool on a wire rack, and get ready to devour.

Baking is my superpower

AND MY APRON
IS MY CAPE.

IF YOU CAN'T CHANGE THE WORLD WITH COOKIES, *how can you change the world?*

SOFT-BAKE FUNFETTI *cookies*

Makes approx. 15
Prep 20 minutes,
plus 1 hour chilling
Cook 8–10 minutes

Ingredients

260 g (9 oz) plain flour
1 tsp baking powder
¾ tsp bicarbonate of soda
pinch of salt
3 tbsp vegan funfetti sprinkles

Ingredients cont.

200 g (7 oz) caster sugar
120 ml (4 fl oz) vegetable oil
60 ml (2 fl oz) water
1 tsp apple cider vinegar
½ tsp vanilla extract

Method

1. In a large bowl, mix together the flour, baking powder, bicarbonate of soda and salt. Stir in the funfetti sprinkles until incorporated.

2. In a separate bowl, combine the sugar, oil, water, apple cider vinegar and vanilla extract, until smooth.

3. Mix the dry ingredients into the wet ingredients until fully combined. Cover the bowl in vegan food wrap and refrigerate for one hour.

4. Preheat the oven to 190°C/170°C fan/gas 5 and line a baking tray with greaseproof paper.

5. Take tablespoon-sized amounts of the mixture and roll into balls, flattening slightly. Place the cookies on the baking tray.

6. Bake the cookies for 8–10 minutes until they're light brown on the bottom. Allow to cool on a wire rack and enjoy with friends (or eat them all yourself – we won't tell!).

JAM
THUMBPRINT
cookies

Makes approx. 15
Prep 15 minutes, plus 30 minutes chilling
Cook 10 minutes

Ingredients

160 g (5½ oz) plain flour
85 g (3 oz) coconut oil, melted
3 tbsp maple syrup
pinch of salt
85 g (3 oz) jam (choose your favourite flavour!)

Method

1. In a medium bowl, mix together the flour, oil, maple syrup and salt. Cover the bowl in vegan food wrap and chill in the fridge for 30 minutes.

2. Preheat the oven to 190°C/170°C fan/gas 5 and line a baking tray with greaseproof paper.

3. Take tablespoon-sized amounts of the mixture and roll them into balls. Make an imprint in the centre of each cookie with your thumb and fill with jam.

4. Bake the cookies for 10 minutes until golden-brown at the edges and cool on a wire rack. Enjoy your jammy treat.

LEMON
cookies

Makes approx. 12
Prep 10 minutes, plus 1 hour chilling
Cook 10 minutes

Ingredients

65 g (2½ oz) fine oat flour
115 g (4 oz) almond flour
2 tbsp tapioca starch
pinch of salt
1½ tsp baking powder
2 tbsp coconut sugar
1 tsp lemon zest
4 tbsp maple syrup
2 tbsp lemon juice
2 tsp vanilla extract

Method

1. In a large bowl, thoroughly mix the flours, tapioca starch, salt, baking powder and coconut sugar. Mix in the lemon zest.

2. Add the maple syrup, lemon juice and vanilla extract, and stir well until the mixture becomes thick and sticky.

3. Cover the bowl with vegan food wrap and refrigerate for one hour.

4. Preheat the oven to 180°C/160°C fan/gas 4 and line a baking tray with greaseproof paper.

5. Roll out the chilled dough to approx. ½ cm–1 cm thick. Use a round cookie cutter to cut out the shapes.

6. Place the cookies on the baking tray and bake for 10 minutes until the cookie edges turn golden-brown. Allow to cool on a wire rack and enjoy. Yum!

BANANA AND CHOC CHIP OAT *cookies*

Makes approx. 20
Prep 20 minutes
Cook 12–14 minutes

Ingredients

1 medium very ripe banana, peeled
75 g (2½ oz) granulated sugar
60 g (2 oz) soft brown sugar
80 ml (2¾ fl oz) grapeseed oil
1 tsp vanilla extract
125 g (4½ oz) plain flour
170 g (6 oz) rolled oats
½ tsp bicarbonate of soda
½ tsp ground cinnamon
pinch of salt
85 g (3 oz) vegan chocolate chips
4 tbsp unsweetened dried coconut

Method

1. Preheat the oven to 180°C/160°C fan/gas 4 and line a baking tray with greaseproof paper.

2. In a medium bowl, mash the banana with the sugars, grapeseed oil and vanilla extract until the mixture is smooth.

3. Stir in the rest of the ingredients then use your hands to fully combine the mixture.

4. Take tablespoon-sized amounts of the dough and roll into balls and flatten slightly. Place the cookies on the baking tray.

5. Bake for 12–14 minutes until the cookies turn golden-brown, and allow to cool on a wire rack. Tuck in!

Life is always sweet with cookies around.

TWO COOKIES FELL IN LOVE WHILE THEY WERE BAKING IN THE OVEN.

IT WAS A BATCH MADE *in heaven!*

CHOCOLATE BROWNIE *cookies*

Makes approx. 22
Prep 20–30 minutes
Cook 10 minutes

Ingredients

60 g (2 oz) vegan butter
100 g (3½ oz) coconut sugar
90 g (3 oz) coconut oil
6 tbsp maple syrup
1 tsp vanilla extract

Ingredients Cont.

95 g (3¼ oz) cocoa powder
2 flax eggs (2 tbsp ground flaxseed & 6 tbsp water,
whisk and set for 15 minutes)
95 g (3¼ oz) oat flour
½ tsp baking powder
pinch of salt
45 g (1½ oz) vegan chocolate chips

Method

1. Preheat the oven to 180°C/160°C fan/gas 4
   and line a baking tray with greaseproof paper.

2. In a pan, melt together the vegan butter, coconut
   sugar, coconut oil, maple syrup and vanilla extract.
   Whisk to combine then remove the pan from the
   heat and set aside to cool a little.

3. Slowly add the cocoa powder to the pan, whisking
   until shiny and smooth. Whisk in the flax egg.

4. In a bowl, sift together the oat flour and baking
   powder, before gently folding into the wet
   ingredients until just combined. Add the chocolate
   chips and mix until combined.

5. Take tablespoon-sized amounts of the mixture and
   roll into balls, flattening slightly. Place on the baking
   tray, leaving space between each cookie.

6. Bake the cookies for approximately 10 minutes,
   allow to cool on a wire rack, and enjoy.

CRANBERRY
AND WHITE
CHOCOLATE
cookies

Makes approx. 24
Prep 20 minutes
Cook 10 minutes

Ingredients

115 g (4 oz) vegan butter
70 g (2½ oz) granulated sugar
70 g (2½ oz) demerara sugar
3 tbsp aquafaba (chickpea water)
195 g (6¾ oz) plain flour
¼ tsp ground cinnamon
½ tsp bicarbonate of soda
75 g (2½ oz) dried cranberries
100 g (3½ oz) vegan white chocolate, chopped

Method

1. Preheat the oven to 180°C/160°C fan/gas 4
   and line a baking tray with greaseproof paper.

2. In a large bowl, beat together the vegan butter
   and sugars until smooth. Mix in the aquafaba.

3. Sift in the flour and add the cinnamon and
   bicarbonate of soda. Mix until a sticky dough
   forms. Fold in the cranberries and white chocolate.

4. Take tablespoon-sized amounts of the mixture
   and roll into balls, then flatten slightly. Place on
   the baking tray with space between each cookie.

5. Bake the cookies for approximately 10 minutes,
   allow to cool on a wire rack, then get stuck in.

MATCHA *cookies*

Makes approx. 24
Prep 20 minutes, plus 2 hours chilling
Cook 15 minutes

Ingredients

260 g (9 oz) plain flour
15 g (½ oz) matcha powder
170 g (6 oz) vegan butter
140 g (5 oz) icing sugar
pinch of salt
1 flax egg (1 tbsp ground flaxseed & 3 tbsp water,
whisk and set for 15 minutes)
½ tbsp black sesame seeds

Method

1. Sift the flour and matcha into a bowl.

2. In another bowl, beat the vegan butter until
   creamy. Add the icing sugar and salt and beat
   until light and fluffy. Mix in the flax egg.

3. Add the flour mixture to the butter mixture
   and mix until combined.

4. Cover the bowl in vegan food wrap and refrigerate
   for two hours.

5. Preheat the oven to 175°C/155°C fan/gas 3
   and line a baking tray with greaseproof paper.

6. Take tablespoon-sized amounts of the mixture
   and roll into balls, flattening slightly. Place on the
   baking tray and gently press the sesame seeds into
   the tops of the cookies.

7. Bake for approximately 15 minutes then allow to
   cool on a wire rack. Enjoy!

CHOCOLATE PROTEIN *cookie* (FOR ONE)

Makes 1 (large)
Prep 10 minutes
Cook 15 minutes

Ingredients

30 g (1 oz) protein powder
2 tbsp oat flour
1 tbsp cocoa powder
1 tbsp coconut sugar
½ tsp ground flaxseed
¼ tsp bicarbonate of soda
pinch of salt
3 tbsp apple sauce
2 tbsp plant-based milk
1 tbsp almond butter
¼ tsp vanilla extract
2–3 tbsp vegan chocolate chips

Method

1. Preheat the oven to 175°C/155°C fan/gas 3 and line a round cake tin with greaseproof paper.

2. In a medium bowl, mix together the protein powder, flour, cocoa powder, sugar, flaxseed, bicarbonate of soda and salt.

3. In a separate bowl, combine the apple sauce, plant-based milk, almond butter and vanilla extract. Mix the wet and dry mixtures until fully incorporated. Fold in the chocolate chips (adding more if you wish).

4. Form the mixture into a ball and slightly flatten it once in the cake tin.

5. Bake for approx. 15 minutes until golden-brown. Allow the cookie to cool a little before removing it from the tin and transferring it to a wire rack to cool completely. Treat yourself to a slice.

My baking is so fabulous, even the smoke alarm cheers me on.

WHEN IN DOUBT,
bake cookies.

RED VELVET
CRINKLE
cookies

Makes approx. 12
Prep 15 minutes
Cook 12 minutes

Ingredients

95 g (3¼ oz) plain flour
½ tbsp cocoa powder
½ tsp bicarbonate of soda
½ tsp baking powder
pinch of salt

Ingredients cont.

60 g (2 oz) vegan butter
70 g (2½ oz) granulated sugar
1½ tbsp maple syrup
1 tbsp plant-based milk
1¾ tsp vegan red food colouring
1 tsp vanilla extract
55 g (2 oz) icing sugar for coating

Method

1. Preheat the oven to 180°C/160°C fan/gas 4 and line a baking tray with greaseproof paper.

2. In a large bowl, mix together the flour, cocoa powder, bicarbonate of soda, baking powder and salt.

3. In a medium bowl, cream together the vegan butter and sugar. Mix in the maple syrup, plant-based milk, food colouring and vanilla extract, until combined.

4. Mix the dry ingredients into the wet ingredients until a dough is formed.

5. Take tablespoon-sized balls of the dough and roll them in the icing sugar until they're completely covered.

6. Flatten the balls slightly on the baking tray.

7. Bake for approximately 10–12 minutes, allow to cool on a wire rack, and eat your creations.

CINNAMON PECAN *cookies* (GF)

Makes approx. 15
Prep 10 minutes
Cook 12 minutes

Ingredients

170 g (6 oz) gluten-free flour
¼ tsp baking powder
½ tsp bicarbonate of soda
¾ tsp ground cinnamon
pinch of salt

Ingredients cont.

90 g (3 oz) coconut oil, melted
130 g (4½ oz) coconut sugar
1 flax egg (1 tbsp ground flaxseed & 3 tbsp water,
whisk and set for 15 minutes)
1 tsp vanilla extract
45 g (1½ oz) pecans, chopped,
plus 15 whole pecans
2–4 tbsp almonds, whole

Method

1. Preheat the oven to 190°C/170°C fan/gas 5
   and line a baking tray with greaseproof paper.

2. In a medium bowl, whisk together the flour, baking
   powder, bicarbonate of soda, cinnamon and salt.

3. In a large bowl, mix together the coconut oil,
   coconut sugar, flax egg and vanilla extract,
   until fully incorporated.

4. Slowly add the dry ingredients to the wet
   ingredients, mixing well, then fold in the
   chopped pecans.

5. Take tablespoon-sized amounts of the mixture,
   roll into balls and flatten slightly. Place on the
   baking tray and gently press the whole pecans
   and almonds onto the tops of the cookies.

6. Bake for approximately 15 minutes, allow to cool
   on a wire rack, and enjoy.

CITRUS
POPPY SEED
cookies

Makes approx. 12
Prep 20 minutes
Cook 13 minutes

Ingredients

350 g (12¼ oz) plain flour
2 tbsp poppy seeds
½ tsp bicarbonate of soda
pinch of salt
120 g (4¼ oz) coconut oil, melted
200 g (7 oz) caster sugar, plus extra for sprinkling
1 tbsp lemon zest
60 ml (2 fl oz) olive oil
1 flax egg (1 tbsp ground flaxseed & 3 tbsp water,
whisk and set for 15 minutes)
2 tbsp lemon juice

Method

1. Preheat the oven to 175°C/155°C fan/gas 3
   and line a baking tray with greaseproof paper.

2. In a medium bowl, mix together the flour,
   poppy seeds, bicarbonate of soda and salt.

3. In a large bowl, mix the coconut oil, sugar and
   lemon zest, until combined. Add the olive oil,
   flax egg and lemon juice, and continue mixing.

4. Add the dry ingredients to the wet mixture and
   mix until incorporated.

5. Take tablespoon-sized amounts of the mixture
   and roll into balls, then flatten slightly. Place on the
   baking tray and sprinkle over the extra granulated
   sugar. Bake for approximately 13 minutes, then
   allow to cool on a wire rack. Mmm!

VALENTINE'S HEART *cookies*

Makes approx. 25
Prep 25 minutes, plus 30 minutes chilling
Cook 10 minutes

Ingredients

230 g (8 oz) vegan butter
300 g (10½ oz) caster sugar
pinch of salt
1 tsp salted caramel extract
3 flax eggs (3 tbsp ground flaxseed & 9 tbsp water,
whisk and set for 15 minutes)
450 g (15¾ oz) plain flour
3 tsp baking powder

Icing

260 g (9 oz) icing sugar
1 tbsp plant-based milk
1 tbsp golden syrup
½ tsp vanilla extract
vegan pink and red food colouring

Method

1. In a large bowl, whip the vegan butter using a stand
   mixer or whisk until it's light and fluffy. Add the sugar
   and salt and cream together. Then mix in the salted
   caramel extract and flax egg until combined.

2. In another large bowl, sift in the flour and baking
   powder. Slowly add to the wet mixture and combine
   until a dough forms.

Continued on the next page.

3. Cover the bowl of dough with vegan food wrap and refrigerate for 30 minutes.

4. Preheat the oven to 200°C/180°C fan/gas 6 and line a baking tray with greaseproof paper.

5. While the dough is being refrigerated, make the icing. In a medium bowl, mix together the icing sugar and plant-based milk. Add the golden syrup and vanilla extract and mix until smooth.

6. Divide your icing into bowls and add desired amounts of your food colouring to make a variety of colours (e.g. light pink, dark pink and red). Put each colour in a different piping bag ready for decorating.

7. Once chilled, roll out the cookie mixture on a lightly floured surface to about ½ cm thickness, and use a heart-shaped cookie cutter to cut out your shapes.

8. Put the cookies on the baking tray and bake for 8–10 minutes until slightly golden. Allow to cool before decorating with the icing.

9. Once cooled, pipe the icing onto the cookies – you could also pipe Valentine's messages or 'VEGAN' on top in a different colour. Set aside and allow the icing to set, then enjoy.

BAKING IS LOVE MADE edible.

CHOCCY TOFFEE *cookies*

Makes approx. 15
Prep 15 minutes
Cook 15 minutes

Ingredients

190 g (6¾ oz) plain flour
1 tsp bicarbonate of soda
pinch of salt
115 g (4 oz) vegan butter
65 g (2½ oz) caster sugar,
plus extra for sprinkling

Ingredients cont.

1 flax egg (1 tbsp ground flaxseed & 3 tbsp water, whisk and set for 15 minutes)
1 tsp vanilla extract
50 g (1¾ oz) vegan toffee, chopped
20 g (¾ oz) vegan chocolate, chopped

Method

1. Preheat the oven to 175°C/155°C fan/gas 3 and line a baking tray with greaseproof paper.

2. In a medium bowl, mix together the flour, bicarbonate of soda and salt.

3. In a large bowl, cream together the vegan butter and sugar, until light and fluffy. Mix in the flax egg and vanilla extract.

4. Add the dry ingredients to the wet mixture and combine thoroughly. Fold in the chopped toffee and vegan chocolate.

5. Take tablespoon-sized amounts of the mixture, roll into balls and flatten slightly. Place on the baking tray and sprinkle the extra sugar on top.

6. Bake for approximately 15 minutes, allow to cool on a wire rack, then indulge with a cuppa.

APPLE
PIE
cookies

Makes approx. 20
Prep 20 minutes
Cook 15 minutes

Ingredients

170 g (6 oz) rolled oats
190 g (6¾ oz) whole wheat flour
150 g (5¼ oz) coconut sugar
1½ tsp baking powder
1 tsp ground cinnamon
pinch of salt
235 ml (8¼ fl oz) plant-based milk
170 g (6 oz) apple sauce
85 g (3 oz) coconut oil, melted
1 tsp vanilla extract
130 g (4½ oz) grated apple
45 g (1½ oz) walnuts, finely chopped

Method

1. Preheat the oven to 175°C/155°C fan/gas 3
   and line a baking tray with greaseproof paper.

2. In a large bowl, mix together the oats, flour, sugar,
   baking powder, cinnamon and salt.

3. In a separate bowl, combine the plant-based
   milk, apple sauce, coconut oil and vanilla extract.
   Pour the mixture over the dry ingredients and
   mix in the grated apple and chopped walnuts.
   Stir together until just combined.

4. Take tablespoon-sized amounts of the mixture
   and spoon onto the baking tray. Bake for approx.
   15 minutes then allow to cool on a wire rack.
   It's cookie time.

CHERRY SHORTBREAD *cookies*

Makes approx. 12
Prep 10 minutes, plus 40 minutes freezing time
Cook 15 minutes

Ingredients

115 g (4 oz) vegan butter
50 g (1¾ oz) granulated sugar
135 g (4¾ oz) plain flour
pinch of salt
40 g (1½ oz) maraschino cherries, chopped

Method

1. In a large bowl, cream together the vegan butter and sugar. In another bowl, sift the flour and salt.

2. Combine the two mixtures and fold in the chopped maraschino cherries.

3. Take the dough out of the bowl and roll it into a log shape, about 4 cm thick. Wrap the log in vegan food wrap and freeze it for around 40 minutes.

4. Preheat the oven to 180°C/160°C fan/gas 4 and line a baking tray with greaseproof paper.

5. Unwrap the cookie dough and cut ½ cm thick slices out of the log with a sharp knife.

6. Place the cookies on the baking tray and bake for approximately 15 minutes. Allow to cool on a wire rack, then devour.

ORANGE CINNAMON CHRISTMAS *cookies*

Makes approx. 22
Prep 15 minutes
Cook 6–8 minutes

Ingredients

215 g (7½ oz) ground hazelnuts
165 g (5¾ oz) soft brown sugar
165 g (5¾ oz) ground almonds

Ingredients cont.

95 g (3¼ oz) plain flour
2 tbsp ground cinnamon
120 ml (4¼ fl oz) water
1 tbsp orange juice

Icing

110 g (3¾ oz) golden icing sugar
1 tbsp plant-based milk, plus extra as needed
½ tsp cinnamon, plus extra for sprinkling

Method

1. Preheat the oven to 180°C/160°C fan/gas 4
   and line a baking tray with greaseproof paper.

2. In a large bowl, add all the dry ingredients and mix
   together, then add the wet ingredients and combine.

3. On a lightly floured surface, roll out the dough
   to about ½ cm–1 cm thick and cut out star shapes
   with a cookie cutter.

4. Place the cookies on the baking tray and bake
   for 6–8 minutes.

5. While the cookies are baking, make the icing.
   In a small bowl, combine the icing ingredients
   until smooth. Once the cookies have cooled,
   spread the icing evenly over them with a palette
   knife and sprinkle with a little extra cinnamon.
   Mmm, delicious!

MY SPECIAL TALENT IS *eating cookies.*

Stressed
is desserts
spelled
backwards.

CHICKPEA AND CRACKED BLACK PEPPER SAVOURY *cookies*

Makes approx. 15
Prep 15 minutes
Cook 25 minutes

Ingredients

80 g (2¾ oz) chickpeas,
drained and rinsed
65 g (2¼ oz) plain flour
30 g (1 oz) semolina flour
10 g (½ oz) ground almonds
45 g (1½ oz) vegan butter

Ingredients cont.

pinch of salt
1 tsp cracked pepper
1 tbsp flaxseed
1½ tbsp black soya bean paste
4–5 tbsp water
2 tbsp black sesame seeds

Method

1. Preheat the oven to 200°C/180°C fan/gas 6 and line a baking tray with greaseproof paper.

2. In a small bowl, roughly mash the chickpeas with the back of a fork.

3. In a large bowl, mix together the flour, semolina, ground almonds, vegan butter, salt, pepper and flaxseed until the mixture resembles breadcrumbs.

4. Add the soya bean paste and mashed chickpeas, mixing well with your hands. Add a little water at a time until a doughy consistency forms.

5. Roll out the dough to approx. ½ cm–1 cm thick and cut out the cookies with a round cookie cutter. Place on the baking tray and sprinkle the sesame seeds on top of each cookie.

6. Bake the cookies for approximately 25 minutes until golden-brown, then allow to cool on a wire rack. They make the perfect savoury treat.

MINI MERINGUE *cookies*

Makes approx. 30
Prep 15–20 minutes
Cook 1½ –2½ hours

Ingredients

120 ml (4¼ fl oz) aquafaba (chickpea water)
¼ tsp vanilla extract
¼ tsp cream of tartar
70 g (2½ oz) granulated sugar

Method

1. Preheat the oven to 100°C/80°C fan/gas 1 and line a baking tray with greaseproof paper.

2. Add the aquafaba, vanilla extract and cream of tartar to a large bowl and beat on high with an electric mixer. As you whip, add the sugar one tablespoon at a time, until stiff peaks form (this may take around five minutes).

3. Spoon small dollops of the mixture onto the baking tray and bake for 1½–2½ hours, checking on them regularly.

4. Once baked to your preferred texture, remove from the oven and allow to cool. Enjoy!

CRANBERRY
AND APRICOT
cookies

Makes approx. 10
Prep 20 minutes
Cook 10 minutes

Ingredients

40 g (1½ oz) dried apricots, chopped
35 g (1¼ oz) dates, pitted and chopped
30 g (1 oz) almond flour
30 g (1 oz) oat flour
½ tsp ground cinnamon
½ tsp baking powder
1 tbsp ground flaxseed
25 g (¾ oz) dried cranberries

Method

1. Preheat the oven to 190°C/170°C fan/gas 5 and line a baking tray with greaseproof paper.

2. Soak the apricots and dates in a bowl of boiling water for 5–10 minutes.

3. Once soaked, strain well and blend in a food processor with a little water, until the fruit is in fairly small pieces.

4. Add the flours, cinnamon, baking powder, flaxseed and cranberries to the processor and pulse a few times until everything is combined, adding a little more water if needed to bring the mixture together. (Take care not to chop everything too much.)

5. Take tablespoon-sized amounts of the mixture, roll into balls and flatten slightly. Place on the baking tray and bake for approx. 10 minutes. Cool on a wire rack, then enjoy your fruity creations.

SPICED PUMPKIN *cookies* (WITH A MAPLE GLAZE)

Makes approx. 20
Prep 15 minutes
Cook 15 minutes

Ingredients

115 g (4 oz) vegan butter
100 g (3½ oz) granulated sugar
50 g (1¾ oz) soft brown sugar
1 tsp vanilla extract

Ingredients cont.

75 g (2½ oz) pumpkin purée
190 g (6¾ oz) plain flour
½ tsp baking powder
½ tsp bicarbonate of soda
1 tsp ground cinnamon, plus
extra for sprinkling
¼ tsp nutmeg
pinch of salt

Maple Glaze

120 g (4 oz) icing sugar
2 tbsp maple syrup
2 tbsp plant-based milk
1 tsp vanilla extract

Method

1. Preheat the oven to 180°C/160°C fan/gas 4
   and line a baking tray with greaseproof paper.

2. In a large bowl, cream together the vegan butter
   and two sugars. Mix in the vanilla extract and
   pumpkin purée.

3. Combine the flour, baking powder, bicarbonate of
   soda, cinnamon, nutmeg and salt in a separate bowl.
   Add to the butter mixture and mix thoroughly.

4. Take two-tablespoon-sized amounts of the mixture
   and roll into balls, flattening slightly. Place on the
   baking tray and bake for approximately 10 minutes.
   Allow to cool on a wire rack.

5. While the cookies are baking, make the maple glaze.
   In a small bowl, mix together the icing ingredients,
   until combined.

6. When the cookies have cooled, use a teaspoon to
   spread the maple glaze on top. Sprinkle with a little
   more cinnamon if you wish.

Today I will live
in the moment.
unless it's
unpleasant,
in which
case I will eat
a cookie!

Cookie Monster

WHY DID THE COOKIE HAVE TO GO TO THE HOSPITAL?

Because it felt crumby.

CHOCOLATE
mint thins

Makes approx. 16
Prep 30 minutes
Cook 10 minutes,
plus 9 hours chilling

Mint Chocolate Dip

400 g (14 oz) vegan dark
chocolate, chopped
1 tsp coconut oil
½ tsp mint extract

Ingredients

112 g (4 oz) vegan butter
100 g (3½ oz) granulated sugar
100 g (3½ oz) soft brown sugar
½ tsp mint extract
125 g (4½ oz) plain flour
55 g (2 oz) cocoa powder
1 tsp bicarbonate of soda
pinch of salt
3 tbsp plant-based milk

Method

1. In a large bowl, cream together the vegan butter and sugars. Stir in the mint extract.

2. Sift the flour and cocoa powder into a separate bowl, then stir in the bicarbonate of soda and salt. Add the flour mixture to the butter mixture, and mix by hand until a crumbly texture forms.

3. Add the plant-based milk, one tablespoon at a time, until the dough is thick.

4. Take the dough out of the bowl and roll it into a log shape, about 4 cm thick. Wrap the log in vegan food wrap and freeze it for around 40 minutes.

5. Preheat the oven to 180°C/160°C fan/gas 4 and line a baking tray with greaseproof paper.

6. Unwrap the cookie dough and cut ½ cm thick slices out of the log with a sharp knife.

7. Place on the baking tray and bake for approx. 10 minutes. Allow to cool on a wire rack.

8. Once the cookies have cooled completely, make the mint chocolate dip. Melt the vegan chocolate in a bowl in the microwave, at 30 second intervals, until smooth. Stir in the coconut oil and mint extract until combined.

9. Coat the cookies in the melted chocolate and place on a lined baking tray. Pop in the fridge overnight, then tuck into your sweet delights.

MOCHA
OATMEAL *cookies*

Makes approx. 12
Prep 20 minutes
Cook 20 minutes

Ingredients

130 g (4½ oz) oat flour
85 g (3 oz) rolled oats
1 tbsp soft brown sugar
1 tsp baking powder
pinch of salt
1 banana, mashed

Mocha

2 tsp instant coffee powder
120 ml (4 fl oz) water
60 ml (2 fl oz) plant-based milk
1 tbsp cocoa powder
4 tbsp maple syrup

Method

1. Start by making the mocha. In a small pan over a medium heat, brew the coffee in the water and pour it into a mug.

2. In a microwaveable bowl, warm the plant-based milk for 30 seconds and whisk in the cocoa powder. Pour the cocoa milk into the mug, stir in the maple syrup, and set aside to cool.

3. Preheat the oven to 175°C/155°C fan/gas 3 and line a baking tray with greaseproof paper.

4. In a large bowl, mix together the flour, oats, sugar, baking powder and salt. Fold in the cooled mocha and mashed banana until thoroughly combined. Allow to rest for approximately three minutes until thickened.

5. Take tablespoon-sized amounts of the mixture and spoon onto the baking tray. Bake the cookies for approximately 20 minutes, allow to cool on a wire rack, and enjoy.

CHOCOLATE AND PEANUT BUTTER SANDWICH *cookies*

Makes approx. 12
Prep 25 minutes
Cook 15 minutes

Ingredients

130 g (4½ oz) plain flour
5 tbsp cocoa powder
1 tsp baking powder
½ tsp bicarbonate of soda
pinch of salt
100 g (3½ oz) caster sugar
55 g (2 oz) soft brown sugar
85 g (3 oz) coconut oil, melted
85 g (3 oz) apple sauce
3 tbsp plant-based milk
2 tbsp maple syrup
1 tsp vanilla extract

Filling

300 g (10½ oz) icing sugar
115 g (4 oz) natural smooth peanut butter
2 tbsp plant-based milk
½ tsp vanilla extract

Method

1. Preheat the oven to 160°C/140°C fan/gas 3
   and line a baking tray with greaseproof paper.

Continued on the next page.

2. In a medium bowl, sift together the flour, cocoa powder, baking powder, bicarbonate of soda and salt until combined.

3. In a large bowl, cream together the sugars, coconut oil, apple sauce, plant-based milk, maple syrup and vanilla. Sift in the flour mixture and mix to combine.

4. Take tablespoon-sized amounts of the dough, roll into balls and flatten slightly. Place on the baking tray and bake the cookies for approximately 15 minutes. Allow to cool on a wire rack.

5. While the cookies are baking, make the filling. In a small bowl, mix together the filling ingredients, whipping until smooth.

6. Once the cookies are cool, spread the icing filling onto the bottom of one half of the cookie batch. Top each iced cookie with an un-iced cookie to make a filled cookie sandwich. Tuck in and don't hold back.

Home is
WHERE THE
COOKIES ARE.

EARL GREY *cookies*

Makes approx. 15
Prep 15 minutes
Cook 10 minutes

Ingredients

20 g (¾ oz) Earl Grey tea leaves
280 g (10 oz) almond flour
½ tsp baking powder
pinch of salt
½ tbsp lemon zest
6 tbsp maple syrup
1 tsp vanilla extract
½ tsp lemon juice

Method

1. Preheat the oven to 175°C/155°C fan/gas 3
   and line a baking tray with greaseproof paper.

2. In a large bowl, mix together the tea leaves, almond
   flour, baking powder, salt and lemon zest. Slowly add
   the maple syrup, vanilla extract and lemon juice,
   whilst stirring, until the mixture is chunky and sticky.

3. Roll out the dough to approx. ½ cm–1 cm thick and
   cut out the cookies with a round cutter. Place on the
   baking tray and bake for approximately 10 minutes,
   then allow to cool on a wire rack. Yummy!

LIME AND
COCONUT
cookies

Makes approx. 20
Prep 15 minutes
Cook 15 minutes

Ingredients

350 g (12¼ oz) large coconut flakes
70 g (2½ oz) almond flour
90 g (3¼ oz) coconut oil
8 tbsp maple syrup
2 tbsp lime juice

Method

1. Preheat the oven to 175°C/155°C fan/gas 3 and line a baking tray with greaseproof paper.

2. Add all the ingredients to a food processor and blend until it comes together to form a soft, sticky dough. If any maple syrup is left at the bottom of the processor, fold it into the mixture.

3. Take two-tablespoon-sized amounts of the dough and roll into flattened circles. Place on the baking tray and bake the cookies for approx. 15 minutes, then allow to cool on a wire rack before devouring.

CHILLI
CHOCOLATE
cookies

Makes approx. 18
Prep 15 minutes
Cook 10 minutes

Ingredients

210 g (7½ oz) plain flour
½ tsp bicarbonate of soda
pinch of salt
½ tsp ground cayenne pepper
¼ tsp ground cinnamon

Ingredients cont.

45 g (1 oz) cocoa powder
115 g (4 oz) vegan butter
85 g (3 oz) caster sugar
85 g (3 oz) soft brown sugar
1 flax egg (1 tbsp ground flaxseed & 3 tbsp water,
whisk and set for 15 minutes)
1 tsp vanilla extract
150 g (5¼ oz) vegan dark chilli chocolate, chopped

Method

1. Preheat the oven to 175°C/155°C fan/gas 3
   and line a baking tray with greaseproof paper.

2. In a medium bowl, mix together the flour,
   bicarbonate of soda, salt, cayenne pepper,
   cinnamon and cocoa powder.

3. In a large bowl, cream together the vegan butter
   and sugars until smooth. Mix in the flax egg and
   vanilla extract.

4. Slowly add the flour mixture to the wet mixture,
   stirring constantly, until just combined. Fold in the
   vegan dark chilli chocolate.

5. Take tablespoon-sized amounts of the mixture and
   roll into balls, then flatten slightly. Place on the baking
   tray and bake the cookies for approx. 15 minutes.
   Allow to cool on a wire rack then get stuck in.

Life is what
you bake it!

LIFE IS SHORT, EAT COOKIES FOR *breakfast.*

ALFAJOR
cookies

Makes approx. 10
Prep 15–20 minutes, plus 10 minutes chilling
Cook 8–10 minutes

Ingredients

4 tbsp coconut oil, softened
4 tbsp maple syrup
1 tsp vanilla extract
1 tsp ground cinnamon
pinch of salt
125 g (4½ oz) almond flour
95 g (3½ oz) tapioca starch
8 tbsp vegan caramel spread for filling
icing sugar for dusting

Method

1. In a medium bowl, combine the coconut oil, maple syrup, vanilla extract, cinnamon and salt. Add the almond flour and tapioca starch and mix, then knead until it forms into a smooth ball.

2. Place the dough on greaseproof paper and roll it out so it's approximately ¼ cm thick. Use a round cookie cutter to cut out your cookie halves then refrigerate for 10 minutes.

3. Preheat the oven to 175°C/155°C fan/gas 3.

4. Transfer the chilled cookie halves (on the greaseproof paper) to the baking tray and bake for approximately 8–10 minutes. Leave to cool completely before adding the filling.

5. Once cooled, spread some vegan caramel spread onto the bottom of one half of the cookie batch. Top each iced cookie with an un-iced cookie to make a filled cookie sandwich. Dust with sifted icing sugar and enjoy.

BANANA NO-BAKE *cookies*

Makes approx. 18
Prep 10 minutes
Cook 10 minutes, plus 2 hours chilling

Ingredients

2 medium bananas, chopped
125 g (4½ oz) vegan chocolate chips
55 g (2 oz) vegan butter
2 tbsp chia seeds
1 tbsp cocoa powder
75 ml (3 fl oz) plant-based milk
pinch of salt
2 tsp vanilla extract
280 g (10 oz) rolled oats

Method

1. Line a baking tray with greaseproof paper.

2. In a medium pan over a low heat, mix together the banana, chocolate chips, vegan butter, chia seeds, cocoa powder, plant-based milk and salt. Heat until the mixture begins to bubble.

3. Using a fork, mash the mixture until smooth, then bring to a boil for a further two minutes. Remove from the heat and stir in the vanilla extract until combined.

4. Stir in the oats until they're coated in the chocolate. Take tablespoon-sized amounts of the mixture and spoon onto the baking tray. Allow to chill in the fridge for a minimum of two hours, until solid. Simple and scrumptious!

Photo Credits